GW00600668

CONTENTS

40cm = 16in   50cm = 20in   60cm = 24in   70cm = 28in   80cm = 32in

HOW TO CHOOSE HEATHERS

This booklet describes a choice of heathers selected from the large number of named cultivars which are listed in nurserymen's catalogues and in publications such as The Heather Society's *Handy Guide to Heathers*.

These 100 heathers are recommended by The Heather Society as a collection of the best heathers of each species and variety. They have been carefully chosen as a result of wide practical experience in different parts of the world and after taking into account the findings of The Heather Society's Trials at Harlow Carr and in the National Collections at the Royal Horticultural Society's Garden, Wisley, Surrey, England; Cherrybank Gardens, Perth, Scotland and the Northern Horticultural Society's Garden at Harlow Carr, Yorkshire, England.

Although some old favourites have been omitted, a serious attempt has been made to combine the outstanding old varieties with those newer introductions which have clearly proved their garden-worthiness.

Before making a choice of plants, it is important to remember that most of the summer-flowering heathers need acid soil conditions. A decision has to be made as to the style of heather garden that is required. Heathers are so versatile that no hard and fast rules can be laid down for the best effects. Beds can be planted to give a dazzling spread of colour for a limited time, or groups of cultivars with different flowering periods will produce a prolonged, if less striking, display. It is possible to make a choice of heathers which will give flowers throughout the year, and by inter-planting coloured foliage varieties with the flowering cultivars, added interest will be provided in the non-flowering periods. In a large garden drifts of 20 or more plants of one cultivar can give a dramatic effect, but it is generally accepted that plantings of groups of 5 or 7 plants will give very satisfactory results. A quite different effect can be created by planting a mosaic of one, two or three of each cultivar in a patchwork pattern. This is more suitable in the setting of a small garden, and because of their compact habit, the winter-flowering *Ericas* are best for this type of planting.

As a general guide, allow five plants to the square metre (or four plants to the square yard) but always aim for variation in height and form by including a tree heath, taller heathers, dwarf conifers or other ericaceous shrubs.

Heathers with yellow foliage

Those requiring a lime-free soil but can be planted in a tub with ericaceous compost.

Calluna vulgaris 'Beoley Gold'	see Page 13
Erica cinerea 'Celebration'	see Page 21

Those suitable for all soils

Erica carnea 'Aurea'	see Page 19
Erica carnea 'Foxhollow'	see Page 19
Erica carnea 'Golden Starlet'	see Page 19
Erica carnea Westwood Yellow'	see Page 21
Erica erigena 'Golden Lady'	see Page 24
Erica x *griffithsii* 'Valerie Griffiths'	see Page 25

Heathers with golden/red foliage

Those requiring a lime-free soil but can be planted in a tub with ericaceous compost.

Calluna vulgaris 'Firefly'	see Page 14
Calluna vulgaris 'Robert Chapman'	see Page 15
Calluna vulgaris 'Sir John Charrington'	see Page 16
Calluna vulgaris 'Sirsson'	see Page 16
Calluna vulgaris 'Wickwar Flame'	see Page 17

Those suitable for all soils

Erica carnea 'Ann Sparkes'	see Page 19
Erica x *darleyensis* 'Mary Helen'	see Page 23

Heathers with grey foliage

All require a lime-free soil but can be planted in a tub with ericaceous compost.

Calluna vulgaris 'Anthony Davis'	see Page 13
Calluna vulgaris 'Kerstin'	see Page 15
Calluna vulgaris 'Silver Knight'	see Page 16
Calluna vulgaris 'Silver Queen'	see Page 16
Calluna vulgaris 'Silver Rose'	see Page 16
Calluna vulgaris 'Velvet Fascination'	see Page 17
Erica tetealix 'Alba Mollis'	see Page 25

Heathers exhibiting coloured foliage in spring

Those requiring a lime-free soil but can be planted in a tub with ericaceous compost.

Calluna vulgaris 'Kerstin'	see Page 15
Erica x *stuartii* 'Irish Lemon'	see Page 25
Erica x *watsonii* 'Dawn'	see Page 26

Those suitable for most soils

Erica vagans "Golden Triumph'	see Page 25
Erica x *williamsii* 'Cow-y-Jack'	see Page 26

Those suitable for all soils

Erica x *darleyensis* 'J.W. Porter'	see Page 23
Erica x *oldenburgensis* 'Ammerland'	see Page 25
Erica x *veitchii* 'Gold Tips'	see Page 26

Semi-double/Double flowered heathers

Those requiring a lime-free soil but can be planted in a tub with ericaceous compost.

Calluna vulgaris 'Annemarie'	see Page 13
Calluna vulgaris 'County Wicklow'	see Page 14
Calluna vulgaris 'Dark Beauty'	see Page 14
Calluna vulgaris 'Elsie Purnell'	see Page 14
Calluna vulgaris 'J.H. Hamilton'	see Page 14
Calluna vulgaris 'Kinlochruel'	see Page 15
Calluna vulgaris 'Peter Sparkes'	see Page 15
Calluna vulgaris 'Red Star'	see Page 15
Calluna vulgaris 'Tib'	see Page 17
Calluna vulgaris 'White Coral'	see Page 17

Those suitable for most soils

Daboecia cantabrica 'Charles Nelson'	see Page 17

Bud-blooming heathers

All require a lime-free soil but can be planted in a tub with ericaceous compost.

Calluna vulgaris 'Alexandra'	see Page 13
Calluna vulgaris 'Alicia'	see Page 13
Calluna vulgaris 'Melanie'	see Page 15

5cm = 2in   10cm = 4in   15cm = 6in   20cm = 8in   25cm = 10in   30cm = 12in

Erica x stuartii 'Irish Lemon'   Erica arborea 'Estrella Gold'

Tree heaths

Those requiring a lime-free soil but can be planted in a tub with ericaceous compost.

Erica arborea **'Albert's Gold'**   see Page 18
Erica arborea **'Estrella Gold'**   see Page 18
Erica australis **'Riverslea'**   see Page 18

Those suitable for all soils

Erica lusitanica   see Page 25
Erica terminalis   see Page 25
Erica x veitchii **'Gold Tips'**   see Page 26

Calluna vulgaris 'Alicia'   Erica terminalis

Heathers with white flowers

Those requiring a lime-free soil but can be planted in a tub with ericaceous compost.

Those suitable for most soils

Those suitable for all soils

Erica x *darleyensis* 'Arthur Johnson'

Erica x *darleyensis* 'White Perfection'

5cm = 2in   10cm = 4in   15cm = 6in   20cm = 8in   25cm = 10in   30cm = 12in

Heathers with 'pink' or 'mauve' flowers

Those requiring a lime-free soil but can be planted in a tub with ericaceous compost.

Those suitable for most soils

Those suitable for all soils

Heathers with 'red' or 'purple' flowers

Those requiring a lime-free soil but can be planted in a tub with ericaceous compost.

Calluna vulgaris 'Alexandra'	see Page 13
Calluna vulgaris 'Allegro'	see Page 13
Calluna vulgaris 'Annemarie'	see Page 13
Calluna vulgaris 'Arabella'	see Page 13
Calluna vulgaris 'Dark Beauty'	see Page 14
Calluna vulgaris 'Darkness'	see Page 14
Calluna vulgaris 'Peter Sparkes'	see Page 15
Calluna vulgaris 'Red Star'	see Page 15
Calluna vulgaris 'Sir John Charrington'	see Page 16
Calluna vulgaris 'Tib'	see Page 17
Erica ciliaris 'Mrs. C.H. Gill'	see Page 21
Erica cinerea 'C.D. Eason'	see Page 22
Erica cinerea 'Pentreath'	see Page 22
Erica cinerea 'Stephen Davis'	see Page 22
Erica cinerea 'Velvet Night'	see Page 22

Those suitable for most soils

Daboecia cantabrica 'Praegerae'	see Page 17
Daboecia cantabrica 'Waley's Red'	see Page 17
Daboecia x *scotica* 'Jack Drake'	see Page 18
Daboecia x *scotica* 'William Buchanan'	see Page 18
Erica vagans 'Birch Glow'	see Page 25
Erica vagans 'Fiddlestone'	see Page 25
Erica vagans 'Mrs. D.F. Maxwell'	see Page 26

Those suitable for all soils

Erica carnea 'Adrienne Duncan'	see Page 18
Erica carnea 'Ann Sparkes'	see Page 19
Erica carnea 'Loughrigg'	see Page 20
Erica carnea 'Myretoun Ruby'	see Page 20
Erica carnea 'Nathalie'	see Page 20
Erica carnea 'Praecox Rubra'	see Page 20
Erica x *darleyensis* 'Furzey'	see Page 23
Erica x *darleyensis* 'Kramer's Rote'	see Page 23

5cm = 2in   10cm = 4in   15cm = 6in   20cm = 8in   25cm = 10in   30cm = 12in

Heathers with bi-coloured flowers

Those requiring a lime-free soil but can be planted in a tub with ericaceous compost.

Erica ciliaris 'David McClintock'	see Page 21
Erica cinerea 'Eden Valley'	see Page 22

Those suitable for most soils

Daboecia cantabrica "Bicolor'	see Page 17

Heathers particularly suitable for patio planting

The following are particularly suitable for planting in patio containers preferably using ericaceous compost.

Calluna vulgaris 'Alexandra'	see Page 13
Calluna vulgaris 'Alicia'	see Page 13
Calluna vulgaris 'County Wicklow'	see Page 14
Calluna vulgaris 'Dark Beauty'	see Page 14
Calluna vulgaris 'Firefly'	see Page 14
Calluna vulgaris 'J.H. Hamilton'	see Page 14
Calluna vulgaris 'Kinlochruel'	see Page 15
Calluna vulgaris 'Sister Anne'	see Page 16
Calluna vulgaris 'White Coral'	see Page 17
Daboecia x *scotica* 'Jack Drake'	see Page 18
Daboecia x *scotica* 'William Buchanan'	see Page 18
Erica carnea 'Ann Sparkes'	see Page 19
Erica carnea 'Aurea'	see Page 19
Erica carnea 'Golden Starlet'	see Page 19
Erica carnea 'Ice Princess'	see Page 19
Erica carnea 'Lake Garda'	see Page 19
Erica carnea 'Nathalie'	see Page 20
Erica carnea 'Treasure Trove'	see Page 21
Erica cinerea 'Celebration'	see Page 21
Erica cinerea 'C.D. Eason'	see Page 22
Erica cinerea 'Eden Valley'	see Page 22
Erica cinerea 'Lime Soda'	see Page 22
Erica cinerea 'Pentreath'	see Page 22
Erica cinerea 'Pink Ice'	see Page 22
Erica cinerea 'Stephen Davis'	see Page 22
Erica x *stuartii* 'Irish Lemon'	see Page 25
Erica x *watsonii* 'Dawn'	see Page 26
Erica x *williamsii* 'Ken Wilson'	see Page 26

Award of Garden Merit, AGM

The Royal Horticultural Society periodically grants Awards of Garden Merit, AGM, to plants which have proven themselves over a period of time to be of outstanding excellence for garden decoration or use, be of good constitution and require neither highly specialist growing conditions or care.

In the case of heathers, they have to have shown that they perform well over about a 10 year period in a number of different locations and be reasonably widely available (at least in the UK). The Heather Society has a direct input to the granting of these Awards, its recommendations being made as a result of national trials, reports from members in various locations and the results obtained from the various National Collections.

In the preparation of this booklet, The Heather Society has taken these Awards into account but has added a number of newer cultivars which do not yet qualify for an Award.

Calluna vulgaris 'Annemarie' ♈

Calluna vulgaris 'Beoley Gold' ♈

5cm = 2in   10cm = 4in   15cm = 6in   20cm = 8in   25cm = 10in   30cm = 12in

THE RECOMMENDED LIST

The recommended list gives details of flower colour, height, average spread and flowering season, to help in the planning of a heather garden.

There are many other good cultivars which can be used to augment or replace others in the list, to make the heather bed an individual creation.

The Heather Society will continue to evaluate new heathers. If worthy and when generally available, they will be included in subsequent editions of this booklet.

Calluna vulgaris 'Alexandra'	The bi-coloured white-crimson buds in August darken with age to deep crimson but never open. thus giving a good show of colour through to December, making it ideal for window boxes as well as gardens. It reaches a height of 30cm and spreads to 40cm.
Calluna vulgaris 'Alicia'	Masses of white buds which fail to open, resulting in a long "flowering" period, from August to December, making it an ideal companion to 'Alexandra'. It has bright green foliage and a compact upright habit, up to 30cm high and 40cm broad.
Calluna vulgaris 'Allegro' ♀	A distinctive plant with an outstanding display of ruby flowers in late summer on dark green foliage. A vigorous but neat plant growing to 50cm high with a 60cm spread.
Calluna vulgaris 'Annemarie' ♀	An outstanding heather producing long sprays of double rose-pink flowers in early autumn on dark green foliage, reaching a height of 50 cm and spreading to 60 cm.
Calluna vulgaris 'Anthony Davis' ♀	The green-grey foliage makes a good foil for the long sprays of white flowers in late summer, reaching 45cm high and 50cm wide. An ideal plant for flower arrrangers.
Calluna vulgaris 'Arabella'	Brilliant blood red flowers in profusion, in late summer on dark green foliage. It has an open erect habit, growing to 30cm and spreading to 40cm.
Calluna vulgaris 'Beoley Gold' ♀	One of the best foliage heathers, having bright golden foliage throughout the year, enhanced by white flowers borne in late summer. Upright plant reaching 35cm high and spreading to 45cm.

Calluna vulgaris
'County Wicklow'
♈

One of the best compact double-flowered cultivars, bearing masses of beautiful pale shell -pink flowers in late summer on dark green foliage. It grows to a height of 25cm and spreads to 35cm.

Calluna vulgaris
'Dark Beauty'

This outstanding plant has semi-double deep cerise flowers, deepening to ruby in late summer, on dark green foliage reaching a height of 25cm and spreading to 35cm.

Calluna vulgaris 'Dark Beauty'

Calluna vulgaris 'Firefly'

Calluna vulgaris
'Darkness'
♈

Masses of attractive crimson flowers, in late summer, in dense spikes on dark green foliage. This neat compact, upright plant reaches a height of 35cm with a spread of 35cm.

Calluna vulgaris
'Elsie Purnell'
♈

This outstanding plant has long beautiful stems of double lavender flowers in late summer on grey-green foliage. Ideal for flower arranging as it reaches a height of 50cm and spreads to 75cm.

Calluna vulgaris
'Firefly'
♈

The lovely terracotta foliage in summer turns to a striking brick red in winter. The deep mauve flowers in late summer give a peach effect when viewed from afar. A distinctive upright habit 45cm in height and spread of 50cm.

Calluna vulgaris
'J.H. Hamilton'
♈

Double deep pink flowers in late summer on dark green foliage. This dwarf plant growing only 15cm high and spreading to 25cm makes it ideal for the smaller garden or for growing in tubs.

5cm = 2in   10cm = 4in   15cm = 6in   20cm = 8in   25cm = 10in   30cm = 12in

Calluna vulgaris **'Kerstin'**

The colourful tips of pale yellow and red in spring give a very pleasing effect on the downy deep lilac-grey foliage. As the tips disappear they are followed by mauve flowers in late summer. A very hardy, vigorous upright growing plant reaching 30cm in height and spreading to 45cm.

Calluna vulgaris **'Kinlochruel'** ♈

This spectacular double white heather flowering in late summer on neat dark green foliage only grows to 25cm high and 40cm wide.

Calluna vulgaris **'Melanie'**

A distinctive plant with long sprays of white buds which fail to open, showing white from late summer through to early winter on dark green foliage. This erect plant grows to 35cm, spreading to 40cm and is ideal for flower arrangers.

Calluna vulgaris **'Peter Sparkes'**

The superb long spikes of double rose-pink flowers in early autumn on dark green foliage makes this an outstanding plant which grows to 40cm spreading to 55cm.

Calluna vulgaris 'Kerstin'   *Calluna vulgaris* 'Red Star'

Calluna vulgaris **'Red Star'** ♈

This spectacular plant bears long sprays of double cerise flowers in late summer and autumn on dark green foliage. It has an open habit and grows to a height of 40cm with a spread of 60cm.

Calluna vulgaris **'Robert Chapman'** ♈

A very popular plant with striking golden orange summer foliage, turning flame red in winter with a height of 25cm and a spread of 65cm. It has lavender flowers in late summer and early autumn. The plant has a rounded compact habit.

Calluna vulgaris 'Silver Knight'

The downy grey foliage, deepening in winter to purple grey, sets off to advantage the lavender flowers in late summer. This neat but vigorous plant reaches a height of 40cm, spreading to 50cm

Calluna vulgaris 'Silver Queen' ♈

Outstanding downy silver grey foliage in summer, turning dark grey in winter with lavender flowers in late summer. The 40cm high plant is broad and spreads to 55cm.

Calluna vulgaris 'Silver Rose' ♈

This plant with its delicate stems of silver grey foliage is outstanding with its lilac-pink flowers in late summer. It has an upright habit reaching to 40cm and spreading to 50cm.

Calluna vulgaris 'Velvet Fascination'

Daboecia cantabrica 'Hookstone Purple'

Calluna vulgaris 'Sir John Charrington' ♈

The long graceful spikes of pale gold foliage tinged orange, are tipped scarlet in autumn, turning bright red in winter then to bronze in spring. The lilac-pink flowers in late summer are an added bonus. Broad upright habit growing to 20cm high and 40cm wide.

Calluna vulgaris 'Sirsson'

Gold foliage in summer turning a bright orange-red in winter, a spectacular plant for cold open aspects. It has pink flowers in late summer and attains a height of 30cm, spreading to 50cm.

Calluna vulgaris 'Sister Anne' ♈

This semi-prostrate compact plant has mauve flowers in late summer on grey-green foliage, which turns to bronze in winter. A low spreading habit, height 10cm breadth 25cm.

5cm = 2in   10cm = 4in   15cm = 6in   20cm = 8in   25cm = 10in   30cm = 12in

Calluna vulgaris 'Tib' ♛	A distinctive plant with double heliotrope flowers from early summer to early autumn on a background of dark green foliage. A rather open spreading habit which grows to 30cm high and spreads to 40cm.
Calluna vulgaris 'Velvet Fascination'	An outstanding plant with striking silver grey foliage, topped with white flowers in late summer. An erect habit reaching a height of 50cm and a spread of 70cm.
Calluna vulgaris 'White Coral'	Spectacular double white flowers in late summer on bright green foliage, which stays bright all through the winter. This plant is compact only reaching a height of 20cm and a spread of 40cm.
Calluna vulgaris 'Wickwar Flame' ♛	A sturdy plant with gold foliage in summer, turning superb shades of orange then red in exposed conditions in winter. The flowers in late summer and autumn are mauve. This vigorous plant reaches a height of 50cm and spreads to 65cm.
Daboecia cantabrica 'Bicolor' ♛	An unusual plant which can sometimes display white, pink and beetroot flowers, some striped, all on the same stem. It flowers throughout the summer and autumn, on mid-green foliage. It can grow to 35cm high and reach 65cm in spread.
Daboecia cantabrica 'Charles Nelson'	This plant has mauve flowers from early summer through to early autumn on mid-green foliage. It is unique in *Daboecias* in that although the first flowers of the season are single, the later ones are double and do not drop when finished. It has an open sprawling habit growing to 30cm high and spreading to 45cm. A fascinating plant.
Daboecia cantabrica 'Hookstone Purple'	This long-flowering plant has large amethyst flowers from early summer through to late autumn on mid-green foliage. It is useful for tall ground cover as it reaches 45cm in height and spreads to 85cm.
Daboecia cantabrica 'Praegerae'	Lovely glowing cerise flowers from early summer to early autumn on mid-green foliage. This plant grows to 40cm in height and spreads to 70cm.
Daboecia cantabrica 'Waley's Red' ♛	The deep glowing magenta flowers from early summer to early autumn have a slight trace of blue, with mid-green foliage. It reaches 35cm in height and has a spreading habit, reaching 50cm.

40cm = 16in   50cm = 20in   60cm = 24in   70cm = 28in   80cm = 32in

Daboecia x scotica 'Jack Drake' ♔

This plant has lovely ruby flowers during the summer on dark green foliage. It has a neat compact habit reaching only 15cm high and 30cm wide, making it ideal for the smaller garden.

Daboecia x scotica 'William Buchanan' ♔

The deep crimson flowers during summer and early autumn on dark green foliage, make this a popular plant. It will continue flowering until the frosts and grows to 35cm high with a spread of 55cm.

Erica arborea 'Albert's Gold' ♔

A spectacular tree heather growing up to 200cm high with bright gold foliage in winter becoming golden green in in summer. The few white flowers are displayed in late spring. Spreading to 80cm.

Daboecia x scotica 'Jack Drake'

Erica arborea 'Albert's Gold'

Erica arborea 'Estrella Gold' ♔

This tree heather with a height of 120cm, has white flowers in profusion during late spring, on lime-green foliage. The new growth is tipped yellow in spring and early summer. Broad (75cm) compact habit.

Erica australis 'Riverslea' ♔

An outstanding tree heath with a height of 120cm, spreading to 85cm. The flowers in late spring and early summer are lilac-pink on dark green foliage.

Erica carnea 'Adrienne Duncan' ♔

This superb plant has deep heliotrope flowers in late winter on dark green foliage tinged bronze. No more than 15cm high, spreading to 35cm.

5cm = 2in   10cm = 4in   15cm = 6in   20cm = 8in   25cm = 10in   30cm = 12in

Erica carnea **'Ann Sparkes'** ♈	The orange foliage of this plant turns crimson in very cold weather with bronze tips during the rest of the year. A compact plant up to 15cm, spreading to 25cm with rose-pink flowers in late winter darkening to heliotrope in early spring.
Erica carnea **'Aurea'**	This plant has golden foliage, with bright orange tips in spring complimented by masses of lilac-pink flowers during late winter and early spring. It has a neat compact habit with a height of 15cm, spread 35cm.
Erica carnea **'Foxhollow'** ♈	The superb yellow and bronze foliage deepens to orange-red in late autumn and winter. A vigorous, spreading plant, reaching 15cm high and 40cm broad. Shell-pink blossoms in late winter and early spring.

Erica carnea 'Golden Starlet'

Erica carnea 'Ice Princess'

Erica carnea **'Golden Starlet'** ♈	The golden yellow foliage glows in summer and turns lime-green winter. The white flowers in late winter and spring makes this plant shine. A neat 15cm high carpet of colour spreading to 40cm.
Erica carnea **'Ice Princess'**	The displays of attractive long spikes of white flowers in late winter and spring are held erect on bright green foliage. It reaches a height of 15cm , spreading to 35cm.
Erica carnea **'Lake Garda'**	The lovely pale pink flowers in late winter and spring are set-off by the dark green foliage. A vigorous spreading habit, reaching 15cm high and 40cm wide.

40cm = 16in   50cm = 20in   60cm = 24in   70cm = 28in   80cm = 32in

Erica carnea
'Loughrigg'
♈

An outstanding plant with rose-pink flowers in late winter and early spring on dark green foliage tinged with bronze. A vigorous plant which grows to 15cm and spreads to 50cm.

Erica carnea
'March Seedling'

An excellent free-flowering plant with pale heliotrope blooms in spring on mid-green foliage. It grows to 15cm high and spreads to 50cm.

Erica carnea
'Myretoun Ruby'
♈

The outstanding deep magenta flowers in late winter and early spring on dark green foliage make this plant an excellent companion to any of the white *carneas* . It reaches 15cm high and 45cm wide.

Erica carnea 'Myretoun Ruby'

Erica carnea 'Rosalie'

Erica carnea
'Nathalie'

Superb purple flowers in winter and early spring against a background of dark green foliage. The deepest and brightest of the *E. carnea* cultivars. A neat, compact habit, reaching 15cm high and 40cm across.

Erica carnea
'Pink Spangles'
♈

An excellent plant displaying large shell-pink blooms in late winter and early spring on mid-green foliage. A vigorous spreading habit reaching 15cm high and spreading to 45cm.

Erica carnea
'Praecox Rubra'
♈

Heliotrope flowers in winter and spring with dark green foliage sometimes tinged brown. Vigorous, reaching 15cm with a semi-prostrate habit spreading to 40cm.

Erica carnea
'R.B. Cooke'
♈

A distinctive plant with masses of pink flowers in winter and early spring on mid-green foliage, reaching 15cm high by 45cm wide.

5cm = 2in   *10cm = 4in*   *15cm = 6in*   *20cm = 8in*   *25cm = 10in*   *30cm = 12in*

Erica carnea 'Rosalie'	Bright pink flowers in winter and early spring with bronze-green foliage. The low upright flowering stems make it suitable for growing in pots. This plant reaches a height of 15cm. and spreads to 35cm.
Erica carnea 'Springwood White' ♉	Masses of white flowers, in winter and spring with bright green foliage. Vigorous trailing habit, making it ideal for hanging baskets, reaching 15cm high and spreading to 40cm.
Erica carnea 'Treasure Trove'	The salmon flowers in late winter and spring on mid-green foliage, are a very distinctive colour break in *E. carnea*. Compact habit and slow growing., reaching 15cm high by 40cm wide.
Erica carnea 'Westwood Yellow' ♉	An excellent compact plant with yellow foliage throughout the year with a few shell-pink flowers, deepening to heliotrope in late winter and early spring. It reaches 15cm high with a spread of 30cm.
Erica carnea 'Wintersonne'	This distinctive plant produces attractive coloured buds on bronze foliage in late summer and autumn, which open to display lilac-pink flowers darkening to magenta in late winter and early spring. The foliage is red-brown. The plant reaches a height of 15cm. and spreads to 35cm.
Erica ciliaris 'Corfe Castle' ♉	This distinctive plant produces long spikes of large bright rose-pink flowers during late summer on mid-green foliage. It reaches a height of 20cm and spreads to 35cm.
Erica ciliaris 'Mrs. C.H. Gill' ♉	A pretty plant with large crimson bells in late summer and early autumn with dark green foliage. This plant grows to a height of 20cm and spreads to 45cm.
Erica ciliaris 'David McClintock' ♉	Very distinctive bicoloured flowers, white at the base with pale beetroot tips in late summer and early autumn on grey-green foliage. Loose open habit, reaching 30cm high and spreading to 45cm. Suitable for planting in a tub with ericaceous compost.
Erica cinerea 'Celebration'	Intense golden foliage in summer and autumn, turning lime-green in winter with white flowers in late summer. An interesting plant owing to the rare combination of white flowers and yellow foliage in this species. Prostrate habit reaching 20cm high and spreading to 40cm.

Erica cinerea **'Cevennes'** ♛	A very good carpeter with mauve flowers in late summer and early autumn on mid-green foliage. Compact spreading habit reaching 30cm high by 65cm wide.
Erica cinerea **'C.D. Eason'** ♛	The bright magenta flowers, in mid to late summer, glow against the backdrop of dark green foliage. It provides neat ground cover, reaching a height of 25cm and spreading to 50cm.
Erica cinerea **'C.G. Best'** ♛	This graceful plant has rose-pink flowers in summer and early autumn on mid-green foliage. It reaches a height of 30cm and spreads to 70cm.
Erica cinerea **'Eden Valley'** ♛	A lovely plant displaying bi-coloured lavender flowers shading to white at the base in late summer and early autumn with mid-green foliage. It has a tidy prostrate habit growing to 20cm high and spreading to 50cm.
Erica cinerea **'Lime Soda'** ♛	An outstanding plant with soft lavender flowers in profusion during summer and early autumn on lime-green foliage. A very attractive plant reaching a height of 30cm and spreading to 55cm.
Erica cinerea **'Pentreath'** ♛	The beetroot flowers look superb against the dark green of the foliage. The plant is a neat carpeter, reaching 30cm in height and spreading to 55cm.
Erica cinerea **'Pink Ice'** ♛	This attractive plant has rose-pink flowers from late summer to early autumn which are shown off beautifully by the dark green foliage. It has a dwarf bushy habit reaching a height of 15cm and a spread of 35cm.
Erica cinerea **'Stephen Davis'** ♛	The intense magenta flowers are produced in profusion throughout the summer on dark green foliage. An erect growing compact plant, reaching 20cm high and 45cm broad.
Erica cinerea **'Velvet Night'** ♛	A striking combination of deep beetroot flowers and dark green foliage make this a colourful summer flowering plant of erect habit. It reaches 25cm in height and spreads to 55cm.
Erica x darleyensis **'Arthur Johnson'** ♛	Beautiful long stems of pink flowers ,which deepen to heliotrope, throughout winter and early spring. The flowers are slightly scented. The mid-green foliage is tipped cream in spring. A tall bushy plant which reaches 60cm and spreads to 75cm.

5cm = 2in   10cm = 4in   15cm = 6in   20cm = 8in   25cm = 10in   30cm = 12in

Erica cinerea 'C.D. Eason'   Erica x darleyensis 'Mary Helen'

Erica x darleyensis 'Furzey' ♈	An outstanding plant with lilac-pink flowers, deepening to heliotrope, in late winter and early spring. The dark green foliage is tipped with cream pink and red in spring. Bushy habit reaching 35cm high by 60cm wide.
Erica x darleyensis 'Ghost Hills' ♈	An attractive plant with pink flowers, deepening with age to heliotrope, in late winter and spring. The light green foliage has cream tips in spring. It grows to a height of 40cm and spreads to 80cm.
Erica x darleyensis 'Jack H. Brummage'	A neat compact plant with bright yellow foliage in summer, turning to deeper gold in winter. The heliotrope flowers are produced in late winter and early spring. It reaches a height of 30cm and spreads to 60cm.
Erica x darleyensis 'Jenny Porter' ♈	The pale lilac flowers in winter and early spring are followed by pronounced pale cream young growth on mid-green foliage. The plant reaches 45cm in height and 60cm spread.
Erica x darleyensis 'J.W. Porter' ♈	Heliotrope flowers in winter and spring on dark green foliage, which is tipped with cream and red new growth in spring. A spectacular plant which reaches 25cm high by 40cm wide.
Erica x darleyensis 'Kramer's Rote' ♈	An outstanding heather with magenta flowers in winter and spring with dark bronze-green foliage, brightening the darkest of winter days. It reaches a height of 35cm, spreading to 60cm.
Erica x darleyensis 'Mary Helen'	The golden yellow summer foliage on this plant bears bronze tints in winter and displays its pink flowers in early spring. The plant grows to 25cm and spreads to 45cm.

40cm = 16in   50cm = 20in   60cm = 24in   70cm = 28in   80cm = 32in   23

Erica x *darleyensis*
'Silberschmelze'

An attractive plant with ashen-white flowers from early winter to late spring on dark green foliage, reaching a height of 35cm and a spread of 80cm.

Erica x *darleyensis*
'White Perfection'
♈

An outstanding plant with pure white flowers, from early winter to spring, with bright green foliage tipped yellow in Spring. A vigorous plant with an erect habit, reaching 40cm high and spreading to 70cm.

Erica erigena
'Golden Lady'
♈

This compact heather has outstanding golden foliage throughout the year with the addition of white flowers in late spring. It is slow growing and reaches 75cm high and spreads to 55cm.

Erica erigena
'Irish Dusk'
♈

A very attractive plant with salmon buds opening to rose-pink flowers in winter through to late spring on grey-green foliage. It has a bushy upright habit and attains a height of 60cm and spreads to 45cm.

Erica erigena
'W.T. Rackliff'
♈

This plant makes an attractive rich green rounded bush, completely covered in white flowers in spring. It is slow growing and reaches 75cm high and spreads to 55cm.

Erica x *griffithsii*
'Heaven Scent'
♈

Scented lilac-pink blossoms in long sprays from summer through to early winter, on dark greyish-green foliage. A vigorous upright habit reaching 100cm and spreading to 60cm.

Erica x *griffithsii* 'Valerie Griffiths'

Erica x *oldenburgensis* 'Ammerland'

5cm = 2in   10cm = 4in   15cm = 6in   20cm = 8in   25cm = 10in   30cm = 12in

Erica x *griffithsii* **'Valerie Griffiths'**	The yellow foliage in summer deepens to a golden yellow in winter, with pale pink flowers in summer and early autumn. A tall bushy plant growing to 40cm high and spreading to 55cm.
Erica lusitanica ♀	An elegant, erect shrub with mid-green foliage. The pink buds open to white flowers from late winter to spring. It reaches a height of 100cm and spreads to 70cm.
Erica mackaiana **'Shining Light'** ♀	Masses of large white blossoms in late summer and early autumn on mid-grey-green foliage. It reaches a height of 25cm and spreads to 55cm.
Erica x *oldenburgensis* **'Ammerland'**	This very attractive plant has soft pink flowers carried on erect spikes during spring with mid-green foliage. The new spring growth is vivid orange. It has a compact habit and reaches a height of 70cm and spreads to 70cm.
Erica x *stuartii* **'Irish Lemon'** ♀	A neat rounded plant grown for the brilliant lemon colour of its new spring foliage, which persists until after flowering starts. The large mauve flowers are borne from late spring to early autumn. It reaches a height of 25cm and width of 50cm.
Erica terminalis ♀	This erect evergreen shrub is hardiest of all the tree heaths. It has lilac-pink flowers from July to November on mid-green foliage. The faded bells provide an attractive russet hue all winter. It grows to 150cm tall and spreads to 100cm. This is an ideal plant for a decorative hedge.
Erica tetralix **'Alba Mollis'** ♀	Attractive white flowers in summer and early autumn on grey-green foliage tipped silver grey. This compact upright plant grows to 20cm and spreads to 30cm.
Erica vagans **'Birch Glow'** ♀	An outstanding plant with masses of deep rose-pink flowers in late summer andautumn, with dark green foliage. It reaches a height of 30cm and spreads to 50cm.
Erica vagans **'Fiddlestone'** ♀	Superb deep cerise flowers during late summer and early autumn on mid-green foliage, reaching a height of 30cm and a spread of 60cm.
Erica vagans **'Golden Triumph'**	A very attractive plant with mid-green foliage which has bright golden tips in spring. The flowers in late summer and early autumn are white. The height is 40cm and breadth 65cm.

40cm = 16in   50cm = 20in   60cm = 24in   70cm = 28in   80cm = 32in

Erica vagans 'Birch Glow'

Erica vagans 'Lyonesse'

Erica vagans **'Lyonesse'** ♛	Abundant white flowers with golden brown anthers in late summer and autumn on bright green foliage. Attains a height of 40cm and spreads to 65cm.
Erica vagans **'Mrs. D.F. Maxwell'** ♛	A most attractive plant bearing masses of deep rose-pink flowers in late summer and early autumn, with dark green foliage. It reaches a height of 35cm and spreads to 45cm.
Erica x *veitchii* **'Gold Tips'** ♛	The bright green foliage of this tree heath is tipped gold in spring. The white flowers appear in late spring and early summer. It reaches a height of 65cm and spreads to 60cm.
Erica x *watsonii* **'Dawn'** ♛	The greyish-green foliage has red tips in spring, turning golden later. The bells are deep pink and appear in late summer and early autumn. Low growing, only reaching 15cm and spreading to 35cm.
Erica x *williamsii* **'Cow-y-Jack'**	The mid-green foliage is tipped a brilliant yellow in spring. The flowers in summer and early autumn are pink. An open spreading plant which reaches 25cm high and spreads to 45cm.
Erica x *williamsii* **'Ken Wilson'**	Clear magenta flowers in summer and autumn, without a trace of blue, fading to shell-pink, with mid-green foliage. Compact spreading habit with a height of 30cm and a spread to 50cm.

5cm = 2in   10cm = 4in   15cm = 6in   20cm = 8in   25cm = 10in   30cm = 12in